Rev Up Your Writing in Procedural Texts

BY AMY VAN ZEE • ILLUSTRATED BY MERNIE GALLAGHER-COLE

Published by The Child's World®
1980 Lookout Drive • Mankato, MN 56003-1705
800-599-READ • www.childsworld.com

ACKNOWLEDGMENTS
The Child's World®: Mary Berendes, Publishing Director
Red Line Editorial: Editorial direction and production
The Design Lab: Design

PHOTOGRAPHS ©: Suttipon Yakham/Shutterstock Images, 6; Shutterstock Images, 12, 18

COPYRIGHT © 2016 by The Child's World®
All rights reserved. No part of this book may be reproduced or utilized in any form or by any means without written permission from the publisher.

ISBN 9781634070676
LCCN 2014959946

Printed in the United States of America
Mankato, MN
July, 2015
PA02261

ABOUT THE AUTHOR

Amy Van Zee is an editor and writer who lives with her family near Minneapolis, Minnesota. She has an English degree from the University of Minnesota and has contributed to dozens of educational books.

ABOUT THE ILLUSTRATOR

Mernie Gallagher-Cole is a children's book illustrator living in West Chester, Pennsylvania. She loves drawing every day. Her illustrations can also be found on greeting cards, puzzles, e-books, and educational apps.

Table of Contents

CHAPTER ONE
Procedural Texts 4

CHAPTER TWO
Writing Recipes 10

CHAPTER THREE
How It Happens 16

Tips for Young Writers 22
Glossary 23
To Learn More 24
Index 24

CHAPTER ONE

Procedural Texts

Do you know how to plant a garden? Play a board game? Make a salad? How did you learn to do these things? Maybe someone showed you. Or maybe you read instructions.

Now imagine that you must write instructions for others. Where would you start? What words would you use? How would you make sure they did the steps in the right order?

In writing, describing how to do something is called a **procedural** text. Procedural texts help people learn how to do new things. For example, they can tell how to bake a cake. Or they can explain how to put together a toy.

Procedural texts have other uses, too. They can explain how something happens. Have you ever read how a tadpole becomes a frog? What about how a chick hatches from an egg? These explanations use a writing style similar to instructions. The writer starts at the beginning of a **process**. Then, the writer takes the reader through each step. The steps are in **chronological** order. This is the order in which things happen.

Procedural texts often include special **transition** terms. These are words to help guide the reader. A set of instructions might begin with *first*. The next step could begin with *next*. And the last step could begin with *finally*. Other transition terms include *before*, *during*, *after*, and *last*. These words help the reader understand

Using chronological order is an important part of writing procedural texts. For example, suppose a writer's first step mentioned frogs and the last step mentioned tadpoles. Just imagine how mixed up you would be!

how the steps relate to each other. Transition terms explain the time and order.

Procedural texts must be clear and simple. Transition terms help the reader know when a new step is beginning. And short sentences make the text easy to read. Procedural texts are often written in present tense. Clear descriptions help the reader **visualize** the process.

Before you begin writing, think about your **audience**. Who will the readers be? What information will they already know? What do you need to tell them? What questions might they have? Are there any missing steps? Answering these questions will help you write an excellent procedural text!

HOW TO SET THE TABLE

Setting the table is a great way to be helpful. Each person will need his or her own place setting. That is a set of dishes and utensils for eating. First, put a dinner plate on the table. It should be a few inches from the edge of the table. Put it right in front of the chair. Then, place a fork to the left of the plate. Next, place a knife to the right of the plate. After the knife is set, put a spoon to the right of the knife. Next, place a water glass right above the knife and spoon. Finally, put a napkin on top of the plate. Repeat these steps for each place setting. Time to eat!

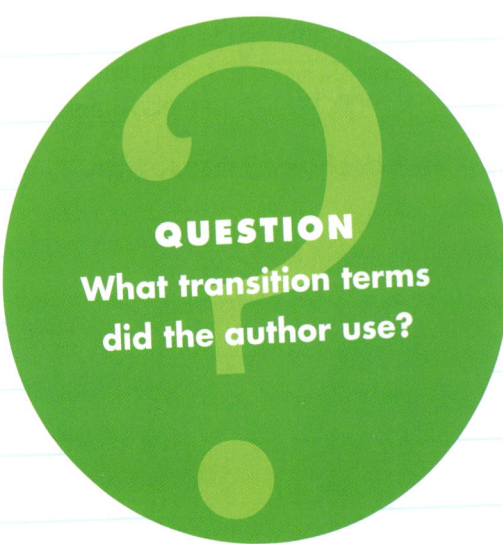

QUESTION
What transition terms did the author use?

CHAPTER TWO

Writing Recipes

What is your favorite food? Maybe it is something spicy such as tacos. Or maybe it is a baked treat such as cookies. Many foods are made by following a recipe. A recipe is another type of procedural text.

Remember that a procedural text describes how to do something. With a recipe, the goal is to help a reader make a certain food. So the writer must carefully describe each step in the process. Details are very important. Be **specific**!

A recipe might start with a short introduction. You could write about how delicious the food is. Or you could suggest other foods to eat with it. Next, you should list each ingredient. Also say how much to use. For example, do not simply write *flour*. Instead, write *1 cup of flour*. It is important to be **precise**. For example, too much butter could make a cake very soggy! Also mention any tools the

Recipes often use transition terms such as *first* or *while*. For example, a cake recipe might tell you to make the frosting while the cake is cooling.

reader will need. The ingredients and tools are listed in the order they are used.

A recipe might look different from other procedural texts. It is often very short. Sometimes a recipe is a paragraph. Other times it uses numbered steps. Each step is very simple. The author writes only one instruction at a time. Each step should be a full sentence.

After writing the recipe, the author should test it. One way to do this is to have someone else follow the steps. Did the food turn out the way it was supposed to? Are there any tricky steps that need to be clearer? If so, the writer will rework those steps. Soon, the recipe will be just right.

PIZZA RECIPE

A pizza is a yummy meal or snack. To make a pizza, you will need a cookie sheet. You will also need a pizza crust, pizza sauce, and a spoon. Finally, you will need shredded cheese and toppings. Your toppings can include pepperoni, onions, and olives.

1. Ask an adult to preheat the oven to 400 degrees Fahrenheit (204°C).
2. Place your pizza crust on a cookie sheet.
3. Use your spoon to spread a thin layer of pizza sauce onto the crust. Keep the sauce an inch away from the edge of the crust.
4. Sprinkle shredded cheese over the sauce.
5. Put your toppings over the cheese.
6. Ask an adult to help you bake the pizza in the oven. Wait about 30 minutes or until the crust is light brown. Enjoy!

QUESTIONS
Where is the list of ingredients and tools? How does having the list there help the reader?

CHAPTER THREE

How It Happens

Have you learned how a bill becomes a law? Or how a plant turns sunlight into food? Procedural texts explain how these things happen. Starting at the beginning, the writer explains each step of the process. Helpful transition terms guide the reader through the stages.

An explanation often includes a short introduction. This tells about the topic. It also says why the topic is important. Just like recipes or instructions, explanations use chronological order. There is a certain **sequence** to the steps. One step will not make sense until the step before it is explained. But unlike recipes or instructions, the reader does not do the steps. Instead, the reader thinks about the steps. The writer could even include an illustration. This will help the reader understand.

Imagine a writer explaining the water cycle. She should make sure the reader knows about different states of water. She might define the words *solid*, *liquid*, and *gas*.

Often, an author is explaining something very specific. It might be a topic the reader does not know much about. So the writer must **define** new words for the reader.

After writing, it is important to **revise**. Read your text again. Make sure all the steps make sense. Each step should contain only one idea. You can add transition terms when the steps are in the correct order. Each step should be clear and simple. When the text is finished, it is a good idea to have another person read it. A new reader can point out any places that are unclear. Revising will help you write strong, clear procedural texts!

BECOMING A BUTTERFLY

How does a caterpillar become a butterfly? There are four main stages of a butterfly's life cycle. The first stage is the egg. The tiny eggs are often green or yellow. The second stage is the larva. A larva is also called a caterpillar. The larva pushes its way out of the egg. It begins to eat a lot of food. It grows quickly. The third step is the pupa. The insect finds a safe place, such as under a branch. It sheds its exoskeleton. This is the outer layer of hard skin. A new shell hardens around the pupa. The pupa is very still. But many changes are happening inside the shell. Wings, legs, and other parts are forming. The fourth stage is the adult butterfly. The adult butterfly breaks out of the hard shell. Its body and wings are soft and wet. In a few hours, the butterfly will be ready to fly away!

QUESTION
What difficult terms did the author define?

TIPS FOR YOUNG WRITERS

1. Start by thinking about the goal of the writing. What would you like the reader to know how to do?

2. Know your topic well. Do lots of research.

3. When writing your steps, think like a reader. Pretend you have never done the steps or heard them before. What questions might you have?

4. Before starting to write a procedural text, brainstorm all the steps. Then work on putting them in the right order.

5. Make sure the steps are listed one at a time. Putting two different instructions in one step could confuse a reader.

6. Look through a cookbook. Pay attention to the way the recipes are written. Maybe you will be inspired to write a new recipe!

7. Use strong verbs to write your recipes, such as *roll*, *pinch*, *drop*, *beat*, *blend*, *sprinkle*, or *mash*.

8. Write as much as you can! Practicing will improve your writing skills and boost your confidence.

9. Find a writing buddy. Have your friend read your work and give you tips for how you can make it clearer.

GLOSSARY

audience *(AW-dee-uhns):* The audience is the person or people who read something. When writing a procedural text, think about your audience.

chronological *(KRAH-nuh-LAH-ji-kuhl):* Chronological means the order in which things happen. A procedural text is written in chronological order to help the reader.

define *(di-FINE):* Define means to tell the meaning of a word. A writer should define any words that the reader might not know.

precise *(pri-SISE):* Precise means exact or specific. When writing a recipe, an author must be precise.

procedural *(pruh-SEE-jur-uhl):* Procedural refers to something that is done in a certain order. A procedural text describes how to do something by following steps.

process *(PRAH-ses):* A process is a series of steps, stages, or actions. When writing a procedural text, the author starts at the beginning of the process.

revise *(ri-VIZE):* Revise means to make corrections or edits to a piece of writing. After writing a first draft, an author should revise the text.

sequence *(SEE-kwens):* A sequence is an order. In a procedural text, there is a certain sequence to the steps.

specific *(spuh-SIF-ik):* Specific means exact and clear. When writing a recipe, the author must be specific with measurements.

transition *(tran-ZISH-uhn):* A transition is a change from one thing to the next. Transition terms, such as *first* or *next*, help readers follow along between steps.

visualize *(VIZH-oo-uh-lize):* Visualize means to picture something in your head. Using strong verbs in a procedural text can help a reader visualize the process.

TO LEARN MORE

BOOKS

Campbell, Cathy. *The Giggly Guide to Grammar Student Edition*. Shoreham, VT: Discover Writing Press, 2008.

Hershenhorn, Esther. *S Is for Story: A Writer's Alphabet*. Chelsea, MI: Sleeping Bear Press, 2009.

Mazer, Anne, and Ellen Potter. *Spilling Ink: A Young Writer's Handbook*. New York: Square Fish/Roaring Book Press, 2010.

Shireman, Myrl. *Developing Science Writing Skills*. Greensboro, NC: Mark Twain Media, 2008.

ON THE WEB

Visit our Web site for lots of links about procedural texts:
www.childsworld.com/links

Note to Parents, Teachers, and Librarians: We routinely check our Web links to make sure they're safe, active sites—so encourage your readers to check them out!

INDEX

audience, 7

chronological order, 5, 6, 17

explanations, 5, 17

illustrations, 17

instructions, 4, 5, 12, 17

introductions, 11, 17

process, 5, 6, 11, 16

recipes, 10, 11, 12, 13, 17

revising, 18, 19

sequence, 17

transition terms, 5, 6, 12, 16, 18–19